D1218902

BRITAIN IN PICTURES
THE BRITISH PEOPLE IN PICTURES

SPORTING PICTURES
OF ENGLAND

GENERAL EDITOR

W. J. TURNER

AUTHOR'S NOTE

This book only attempts to be an introduction to the great school of English
Sporting Painters. I must pay tribute here to Walter Shaw Sparrow's great
books on this subject on which I have largely drawn. I am indebted to the
Duke of Westminster, Mrs. Macdonald-Buchanan of Cottesbrooke, and Mrs.
Taylor of Cheam for putting their houses and pictures at our disposal in
these difficult times, and must also thank generous publishers and owners
for their help.

SPORTING PICTURES
OF
ENGLAND

GUY PAGET

WITH
12 PLATES IN COLOUR
AND
21 ILLUSTRATIONS IN
BLACK & WHITE

COLLINS · 14 ST. JAMES'S PLACE · LONDON
MCMXXXXV

PRODUCED BY
ADPRINT LIMITED LONDON

PRINTED IN GREAT BRITAIN BY
THE SUN ENGRAVING CO LTD LONDON AND WATFORD
ON MELLOTEX BOOK PAPER MADE
BY TULLIS RUSSELL & CO LTD MARKINCH SCOTLAND

LIST OF ILLUSTRATIONS

PLATES IN COLOUR

WINDSOR GREYS AT ASCOT
Oil painting by A. J. Munnings, P.R.A.

SUNRISE ON THE CORNISH MARSHES
Oil painting by Charles Simpson, R.I.

BLACK AND WHITE ILLUSTRATIONS

THE LAST HORSE RACE RUN BEFORE CHARLES II AT DORSETT [DATCHETT] FERRY, 1684
Etching by Francis Barlow, 1687

ORIGINS OF BRITISH SPORTING PAINTERS

THOSE who wish to understand England and its growth during the seventeenth and eighteenth centuries cannot do better than study the sporting pictures of that period. They give as true a picture as the history books of Green or Macaulay. They are essentially English, in fact they form the first English School of painting. Most painting in England before 1660 and much of it for some time after was done by foreigners and a handful of their pupils. The great artists associated with English painting, Holbein, Van Dyck, Lely, Kneller, Van Wyck, were all foreigners, as were many founder members of the Royal Academy in 1768.

The earliest English sporting painters owe much to foreign teachers. There were no others. To the Dutch we owe the introduction of outdoor games into polite society; the only one generally played by the great before the Restoration, unconnected with the practice of arms, was "real" tennis, and *The Gentleman's Recreation*, published in 1686, in all its five hundred folio pages makes no mention of a single game. Our earliest knowledge of football, cricket and other games is from statutes forbidding them, since they distracted the common people from the practice of archery and quarter staff. On the other hand the Flemish school of the seventeenth and eighteenth centuries gives us glimpses of many games played on the ice and village greens of Flanders by both rich and poor. King Charles II introduced pall-mall on his return from Holland and to him we owe organised racing both at Newmarket and Windsor Great Park; though in his time it took place at Datchett Ferry instead of on Ascot Heath to which place it was moved by Queen Anne.

The continent of Europe was two hundred years ahead of this island in matters of art. England had not started building Renaissance houses, when those in Italy and France were mellowed with age. From 1400 to 1500 England was continually torn asunder by civil strife which overlapped the Hundred Years War with France. Feudalism had devoured itself and a new class ruled, men who had made fortunes in cities by trading with both sides and the descendants of ennobled lawyers enriched by abbey lands.

But it was not till Henry VIII dissolved the monasteries, that the nobles realised that a Norman Castle was not the acme of comfort and began to convert the semi-fortified monasteries into dwelling houses. By the time of Elizabeth and James I, they were building mansions more for comfort than protection. The Great Rebellion interrupted this process and Oliver Cromwell realising that castles were incompatible with central government, destroyed or dismantled the vast majority.

Versailles had set the example of vast magnificence. Louis XIV had decorated it with battle pictures and fair women. Now the average Englishman likes fair women but the last thing he desired in his new home, was to be reminded of war. Still the walls looked dull and cold with only plaster decoration. England had ever been the land of the horse and the hound. The Romans had imported British hounds and decked their triumphs with them; even before the Tudors, stallions had been imported from Asia, North Africa and Europe to improve the native breed and a pack of hounds was still an essential part of a nobleman's establishment. Finally, Charles II placed racing on a national basis. All these causes particular to England now called for a particular English form of art. At first the supply was crude.

Some ten years after the Restoration, Francis Barlow originated English Sporting Prints. Fifty years later Wootton was painting masterpieces at Badminton, Althorp and Longleat. By 1783, Stubbs had painted *The Grosvenor Stag Hunt* at Eaton, *Training, Hunting and Shooting* at Goodwood, and at Wentworth its famous frieze of racehorses. He published his *Anatomy of the Horse* in 1766.

In the greatest private collections of the old nobility, sporting pictures have always been allotted a large and prominent place. His Majesty the King has inherited from his forbears one of the most representative collections in the world. In spite of this, the Royal Academy, from its start, has always frowned on sporting art. Not ten per cent. of its best exponents have been admitted to even the outer court of the Academy and it is hard for a sporting picture to pass through its portals. Is it because the Englishman has made up his mind that the foreigner can do certain things better, that it is thought a painter must have learnt his art anywhere but at an English school? Yet without this school,

8

GREY ARAB STALLION

From the original oil painting by John Wootton, c. 1687-1765

THE GROSVENOR STAG HUNT

From the original oil painting by George Stubbs, A.R.A., 1762

we would never have known how the common people dressed or amused themselves, how the plumed sombrero of Charles I became the top-hat of the Prince Consort, or the horses of the reign of Charles II evolved the mighty Ormonde and Manifesto, or how the shooting dog and even our present-day hounds became what they now are from the running and hunting dogs of the Plantagenets. The record of the gradual change from the open fields to the enclosed country would be for ever lost. Neither would we know the stages our race-meetings have travelled from simple little gatherings near Datchett Ferry in the 1680's to the pageant of present day Ascot; how hawking was conducted would have vanished from our ken, and the differences in the conduct of a shoot two hundred years ago.

. During the eighteenth century the breeding of horses, dogs, cattle, sheep and pigs had taken the place of war and had become the ruling passion of the country gentleman; with this went a love for country life, shooting, hunting, racing, gardening. But for this passion, Whitehall might have become a Versailles and wealth and fashion might have been concentrated in London as in Paris. But in England, even the government of the country had to give way to it, and the sittings of Parliament were regulated by the shooting and hunting seasons. In England alone the real home of the ruling class is in the country, not in the capital, from the monarch to the well-to-do tradesman.

Early in the eighteenth century the demand sprang up for portraits of race-horses, hunters and hounds, followed by those of cattle and sheep. As the breeds of the latter improved (and nearly every county had its own special breeds) so the breeder wished them to be more widely known, to add both to his fame and profit, and so the sporting artists of the seventeenth century evolved this most profitable, if not highest, form of art.

THE NATURE OF BRITISH SPORTING ART

THE term Sporting Art covers three distinct kinds of pictures. First, the subject picture largely imaginary but founded on fact, such as Alken's *Hunt Scurry*; second, the illustration depicting some particular scene as true to the actual event as possible, such as Pollard's *King's Birthday*; third, the portrait of an animal with or without human figures, such as Ben Marshall's *Tom Oldaker*. All three overlap in many instances and some pictures contain all three elements.

Sir Francis Grant's *Quorn Hunt at Borough Hill* is a good example of the last. Here we have a fine landscape with the Quorn Hunt moving off to draw, but the arrangement of the figures is purely imaginary, while each horse and human is a carefully drawn portrait compiled from individual sketches or painted direct into the actual design from life. On the other hand, I should call Stubbs' *Shooting at Goodwood* and Boultbee's *Mr. Packe at Prestwold after Partridges* portraiture and illustration only, and Ferneley's *Quorn Hunt at Kirby Gate* is portraiture and imagination. No hard and fast line can be

9

TWO ROYAL SADDLE HORSES AND ANDERSON THEIR GROOM
Oil painting by George Stubbs, 1793

drawn. The introduction of a gun or rod, a dog or dead bird does not make a portrait a sporting picture, though Wootton's portrait of *Tragonwell Frampton* and Marshall's of *Gully* and *Jackson* undoubtedly are sporting pictures. Every line of them breathes of sport.

What is the reason that sporting pictures have been so neglected by the average collector and art critic? Before a man can sit down to paint a hunting run on any scale, he must be master of landscape painting; he must know the anatomy not only of man, but of horse, hound and quarry; he must possess a lively imagination, a good memory of how animals look as they move and a sense of design (an unteachable quality), not only of his landscape but of how to blend his subject into it. Many of the greatest animal painters, including Stubbs and Marshall, got other men, sometimes R.A.s, to do their landscapes, but the results do not come up to the best of either. Above all the artist must have an intimate knowledge of the sport he depicts—in fact, he must have hunted quite a lot. The slightest inaccuracy, even a spur too high or too low, will arouse the suspicion of the sportsman, who will at once look for further slips. Thus the sporting artist has to please many different critics, each ignorant of three-quarters of his difficulties and each looking for some fault in the realm they do understand. Is it surprising if the artist should sometimes fail to please them all?

The average collector is a self-made man, who collects because he has not inherited. As a rule he starts late in life and therefore has no real understanding of sport. His taste must be guided by others. The average sportsman is not as a rule an art connoisseur. He may like sporting pictures, either because he has always been brought up amongst them or because they recall some of his happiest hours, but very few will be able to explain their artistic merit to a non-sportsman. The Royal Academy, as I said before, has always looked down on the animal painter. Yet Stubbs got as much for his pictures as Reynolds. Stubbs could paint a man or woman as well as Sir Joshua Reynolds, but Sir Joshua could no more have painted *Lady Lade* or *The Hambletonian* than Crome or Wilson could have painted *Master Bunbury*. Benjamin West, P.R.A., could paint *The Death of General Wolfe* but never Wolstenholme's *Essex Harriers*. So it has gone on, till at long last in Munnings they have

DARK BROWN HUNTER "CURRICLE" LED BY A GROOM IN ROYAL LIVERY
Oil painting by Ben Marshall, 1767-1835

elected a sporting P.R.A. Sir Edwin Landseer declined the honour in 1868, but he was an animal painter, not a real sporting artist. Sir Francis Grant was elected for his portraits.

So the embryo collector will not be advised to buy sporting pictures by the R.A. If he turns to the picture dealers and the sale rooms, he too often cannot differentiate between what is good and what is just expensive. Being business men, dealers buy what they understand and that is not sport as a rule, though one or two have very fine collections. The collector will be advised to buy Italian, Dutch, French, Spanish and even English eighteenth-century portraits but never sporting pictures. So until Americans, whose fathers had brought them up to appreciate good pictures, came over here to hunt, race and shoot, some of our greatest pictures went for a song. The Americans quickly altered all that, however, and some of the best collections of sporting pictures are to-day in North and South America.

Another difficulty which presents itself to the lover of sporting pictures is that the vast majority are in private hands. It is only during the last few years, with the exception of the Walker Art Gallery in Liverpool, that public galleries have possessed any. To see the best, or even second-best, requires much travel and many private introductions. One must go to Althorp and Welbeck to see Wootton, to Wentworth for Stubbs, Cottesbrooke and Ashwardby for Marshall and Ferneley, Cheam for Wolstenholme, into Essex to see Mr. Gilbey's collection of fishing pictures and to Raby Castle for Chalon. In all these places there are other masters of the English school, but it will take a journey lasting a month to get any real idea, for I have only mentioned a few of the greatest collections; there are Goodwood, Petworth, St. Ann's, Badminton and a hundred more I could name. His Majesty the King's collection of sporting pictures is unfortunately hung in the private apartments, not open to the public.

I am glad to say that our public galleries have at last woken up and are now alive to their past neglect. The Tate Gallery has appealed to the public for gifts of sporting pictures to supplement its meagre collection. The Walker Art Gallery has accepted the bequest of a fine private collection and Mr. Walter Hutchinson hopes to found a Gallery of National Sports and Pastimes.

The end of this war will see the closing of many great mansions and the dispersal of the accumulated treasures of generations, so there should be no difficulty in forming a really worthy collection of this greatest English School. One curious fact about this School is that though essentially English, many of the artists were of foreign extraction whose fathers sought these shores for religious liberty and whose sons found expression of what they sought in depicting the freedom of the English countryside and its sports. In the case of the Sartoriuses, Alkens and Herrings, they handed their gift down for three generations. Chalon, Reinagle, Laport, bear foreign names. But with the exception of a school of Londoners, who flourished round the engraver, John Raphael Smith, about 1775, the great majority were English country-breds.

By courtesy of Captan and the Hon. Mrs Macdonald-Buchanan

GREY STALLION AND MARE

From the original oil painting by Ben Marshall, 1767-1835

EPSOM RACES

Aquatint by C. Hunt after James Pollard, 1772–1867

FRANCIS BARLOW, c. 1626-1704, is the father of English Sporting Pictures. No artist could have been born at a worse time. His prime coincided with the Great Rebellion and the Commonwealth and his maturity with the unsettled period between the Restoration and the accession of Queen Anne. The old nobility had not recovered their equilibrium or the new found their stability.

Barlow did great pictures of birds for Denzil Onslow and for the Drakes of Shardeloes; he designed General Monck's hearse and painted pictures of his lying-in-state and funeral, but what he is most famous for is his sporting prints. These came out in *Several Ways of Hunting, Hawking and Fishing in the English Way*, 1671, etched by Hollar and Bullard and in Bloom's *Gentleman's Recreation*, 1686, the best of which he etched himself. These were followed by *The Last Horse Race run before Charles II at Dorsett Ferry*, 1684. His spelling is even more original than my own. I long suspected "Dorsett" to be a mis-spelling for "Datchett" and this has been confirmed by Sir Owen Morshead, the learned librarian of Windsor Castle.

Where Barlow learned to paint is unknown, but it is impossible to look at his bird pictures without being struck by their likeness to Hondekoeter's. His friends and engravers, Faithorne and Hollar were forced to flee the country after the fall of Basing House, but we have no knowledge of Barlow's whereabouts until 1651, when both he and Faithorne are known to have been living at the Drum, Drury Lane. John Evelyn, the diarist, refers to him as a famous painter in 1656. One of his most interesting pictures is Lord Onslow's *Hunting the Hare with Southern Hounds*. The hounds are nearly life-size, judging by the hare which has caught them up owing to their dwelling and pottering on her line. He also illustrated an edition of Aesop's *Fables* which he published at his own risk, but nearly the whole edition was burnt in the Great Fire of 1660. He left no direct successor, yet, though not in the highest class, he was the best engraver, bird painter and illustrator England had so far produced.

John Wootton, c. 1686-1765, was the next important sporting artist, and could hardly have come under Barlow's personal influence though his books would have been familiar to him. Wootton studied under Jan Van Wyck (John Wyck) until Van Wyck's death at Mortlake in 1702. After his return from Italy, where he went on the advice and with the assistance of the Duke of Beaufort, Wootton struck out in a style of his own. He was joined by James Seymour (1702-1752) a one-time well-off amateur and by Peter Tillemans, a Dutchman. These three worked together for several years and each had a style of his own though they were in many respects similar.

Lord Hylton possesses a *Race at Newmarket*, signed by Seymour; Knoedler sold a picture with an identical background signed by Wootton; yet the backgrounds are in the style of neither, but in the continental manner of Battle

Pieces perfected by Tillemans. There can be little doubt that these two English gentlemen turned artist, spent their time racing and hunting, while the industrious young Dutchman did the donkey work. Seymour's pictures are valuable for their minute detail; the tongue of a buckle is not too small for his attention. He had the reputation of getting a better likeness of a horse than Wootton, who is said to have sacrificed truth to beauty. If this is correct, having regard to some of Seymour's early efforts, perhaps he should be forgiven !

Wootton was the friend of the Dukes of Beaufort, Richmond and Marlborough (Spencer); the Earls of Oxford (Harley of Welbeck) and Devonshire. He was patronised by Queen Anne and George I. The third Duke of Marlborough devoted the whole of his great new hall at Althorp to his pictures. The Duke of Portland has the best collection of Wootton's pictures, the pick of forty-eight painted for his ancestor, Lord Oxford; Lord Spencer possesses Wootton's two largest hunting pictures—thirty feet by ten feet. He and Seymour may be said to have been the pioneers in the straightforward portraiture of horses and hounds. It is through their work that we are able to see to-day the foundation stock of our thoroughbreds. The standards and conventions established by Wootton have been handed down in unbroken apostolic succession to Alfred Munnings and Lionel Edwards. Very few of either Wootton's or Seymour's works have ever been reproduced as prints.

The next great animal painter, probably the greatest, was George Stubbs of Liverpool, 1724–1806. His *Anatomy of the Horse*, 1766, revolutionised animal painting. With the help of Lord Grosvenor of Eaton, Chester, young Stubbs went to Italy in 1754 to study the old masters, but he preferred nature. On his way back, via Morocco, he saw a lion attack and kill a horse. This incident was indelibly impressed on his mind and he introduced it into many of his pictures.

He was an anatomist from childhood. At twenty-one he was lecturing on anatomy at York Hospital and he was engaged in 1750, by Dr. John Burton, to do forty drawings to illustrate a book on midwifery. With his usual thoroughness he "snatched the body" of a newly dead mother and executed eighty drawings from it. Finding no one to etch them, he learnt the trade and did them himself. Having made money with his brush, he retired to a farm, where he carried dead horses up to the attic with the assistance of Mary Spencer, his life-long companion and mother of George Towneley Stubbs, who engraved many of his pictures. His industry was not appreciated by his neighbours, who said he made the district smell like a battlefield, and at the end of two years were glad to see the end of him.

In 1771, urged on by George Cosway, the miniaturist, he abandoned painting for eight years and experimented with enamels which would stand firing and last, not fade and sink, which Reynolds' colours were already beginning to do. Having discovered nineteen colours, he sought a medium to receive them. He tried copper. Lord Melbourne gave him a hundred guineas

A STAG HUNT

Oil painting by John Wootton, c. 1686-1765

for his first effort. Then for years, with the great potter, Josiah Wedgwood, he experimented with porcelain. At last they produced a plaque 40½ inches by 29½ inches and Stubbs threw his invention open to his brother artists. In 1780 he was elected an A.R.A. and in the next year full R.A. He celebrated it by sending in four of his plaques. The R.A. skyed them. Stubbs refused to send in his diploma picture so never actually received his diploma and cold-shouldered the R.A. for ever after. His work is unmistakable. His "signature-tune" is a dock leaf but, like Reynolds, he signs his pictures all over. There is strength and weight in them attained by few; his modelling is superb. His landscapes and middle distances are often weak and this I attribute to short sight brought on by too long hours engraving. This too I believe is the reason that so many of his subjects are "falling out of their canvas" for lack of fore-ground: he sat too close to his subject. His greatest pictures are *The Grosvenor Stag Hunt* at Eaton, *Lord Rockingham's Racehorses* at Wentworth, and the *Hambletonian*, life-size, at Wynyard. In 1943, at Christie's, four very ordinary pictures of his belonging to Lord Bolingbroke, fetched £10,000.

The plaques were not Stubbs's only excursion into ceramics. Most of the hunting scenes on Liverpool "transfer" china are after Stubbs and the raised hunting scenes on Staffordshire beer mugs and jugs are his work. He designed club buttons and the horses on Wedgwood's china. Stubbs might have been a great surgeon, a great potter or a great chemist but he chose to be a great artist and he died comparatively poor. His influence

15

was marked on all his contemporaries : Boultbee, Reinagle, Sawrey Gilpin, all made the greatest possible use of his *Anatomy*, as did the succeeding generation; in fact Ben Marshall and James Ward occasionally suffered from an ill-digested dose of the *Anatomy*.

After Stubbs, the man who probably had most influence on sporting art was a Leicestershire squire, Charles Loraine Smith, 1751-1835, of Enderby in the purlieus of Charnwood Forest, M.P., J.P., poet, deputy master of the Quorn, painter, fiddler, jack-of-all-trades. By the end of the eighteenth century Melton Mowbray was the metropolis of the sporting world, and Enderby the common meeting ground of sporting art and the "noble science."

Boultbee 1753-1812, a pupil of Reynolds and Stubbs, Ben Marshall, 1767-1835, John Ferneley, 1782-1860, and his sons, Clifton Tomson, born 1775, were all bred in the Quorn country; while Henry Alken, 1785-1851, and George Morland, 1763-1804, actually helped the squire with his pictures. The Pollards and Sartoriuses did many pictures of Leicestershire hunts and hunters and amateurs such as Bunbury, Sir R. Frankland, Dean Paul and W. P. Hodges were *habitués* of both Enderby and Melton.

True, the squire was away back amongst the selling platers, when it was flat drawing and painting, but over the sticks of design and imagination, he was right up in the Grand National class at about 11 st. 7 lbs. This is proved by comparing some of his original pictures with Morland and Alken's re-drawings of them. He was a man of strong character and decided ideas of his own. Even if the artists themselves had no high opinion of his painting, their patrons would have, for did not the squire know both ends of the game, and would they not, therefore, ask the artist whom he recommended to immortalise them and their horses ?

George Morland was a wild genius of humble origin. His father was an artist of some repute but went bankrupt. As quite a young man, George aspired to be a buck and mix with that raffish crew of so-called "gentlemen." His own descriptions of his jockeyship at Mount Pleasant and Margate are amusing in their self-revelation !

"'Twas a four mile heat and the first three miles I could not keep the horse behind them, being so spirited an animal by that means he soon exhausted himself, and I soon had the mortification to see them come galloping past me hissing and laughing, while I was spurring his guts out. A mob of horsemen then gathered round telling me I couldn't ride, which is always the way if you lose a heat; they began at last to use their whips. But, however, I did not fare near so well at Margate Races and was very near being killed. I rode for a gentleman and won the heat, the other horses being nearly half a mile behind, upon which nigh four hundred sailors, smugglers and fishermen set on me."

Note the spoilt child, self-pity and someone else to blame for his appalling inefficiency.

GENTLEMAN ON BLACK PONY
Oil painting by Charles Towne, 1763-1840

Morland's drawings and paintings were immensely popular and brought him in large sums but never enough. He loved to be king of his company; any company, so long as he was king. He didn't care what he spent or on whom. All the "legs" of the town were soon on his track, tempting him from his work to buy them and himself drunkenness.

He married a sister of William and James Ward. James married Morland's sister and John Raphael Smith also married a Ward sister. They were joined by Rowlandson, who was a few years older than Morland but had a far from controlling influence on him. With Samuel Howitt and Julius Caesar Ibbetson they formed the London School. Born between 1752 and 1768, with the exception of James Ward, they were all dead by 1827. Morland was utterly unscrupulous. He signed his name to his pupils' work; he accepted payment for a picture from one and sold it next day to another; when pressed by the first, he would do a bad replica, cursing the whole time he was doing it, as if he was the injured party. His regular dealers stood over him with the door key in one hand and a fourpenny bottle of

DICK KNIGHT BAGGING THE FOX
Water colour by C. Loraine Smith, Esq., of Enderby, 1794

gin in the other, till their order was finished and they took it away wet.
Fortunately, at the height of his power, his debts amounted to over £3,700,
so he had to "shoot the moon." Loraine Smith found him a refuge first in
his own house and then at a farm in the neighbourhood. Cut off from his
bad companions and worse liquor, surrounded by the beauties of Charnwood
Forest, he did some of his best work. Thatched cottages, the oak beamed
interiors, the granite-strewn hillside and rides are still there just as he painted
them. If you are familiar with the colour of Charnwood granite and Swith-
land slates, you can easily pick them out : I put these years from 1794 to
1796. His debts squared, he returned to London and his evil ways and died
a drunken pauper at the age of forty-one, in 1804. It is as impossible to
distinguish a bad Morland from one of his school pupil's as to confuse a
good one. Morland was, in his lifetime, and still is the most popular English
artist on the Continent, especially in France; so much so, that many of his
shooting prints have both English and French titles.

None of this school were, strictly speaking, sporting artists. They were
painters of country scenes, into which sport and animals entered. They
saw magic, where the countryman only saw decay. What was wonderful
to them was commonplace to him.

Ben Marshall, 1767-1835, studied under L. F. Abbott as a portrait painter,
but was so impressed with Sawrey Gilpin's 1793 Academy picture, *The*

18

Death of a Fox, that he turned from human to animal painting. Strictly speaking Ben Marshall remained a portrait painter and a very good one too. He is not essentially a sporting artist. The portrait comes first and the sport second. The arrangement of his hounds in his big hunting pictures gives away the fact that he was not a hunting man. I have never seen a hunt scurry (Shire word for fast fox hunt) by him. He never gets his hunt beyond the meet. Writing in 1796, Farington, the gossiping diarist, rates him above Stubbs. Stubbs was then 72, Ben 29. One was starting where the other was leaving off. Ben had an academy education; Stubbs was self-taught. Ben was able to study the *Anatomy of the Horse;* Stubbs had only written and illustrated it! Ben Marshall is a brilliant colourist and a powerful delineator of character. To look at his portraits of Gully and Gentleman Jackson or of himself and Goodson convince one that his horse and hounds are just as true. He lays on his paint extremely thin. He puts real sunlight on the coats of his horses. They don't shine, they reflect. As for truth, you have but to examine *Lord Sondes and His Brothers with the Pytchley Hounds, at Rockingham Castle.* Did you ever see such a scratch lot outside Mr. Wilton's emporium ! There is scarcely a couple out of the same litter.

SIR MARK SYKES' HOUNDS BREAKING COVER
Oil painting by H. B. Chalon, 1771-1849

Look at that big jolly mongrel on the left, the whippets in front on the right. You can pick out the two and a half couple he got from the Squire ! One can understand the two Belvoir hounds top right "offing it" on their own. The proud owner had only collected, or better, "got them together" the summer before to hunt the Pytchley woodlands. Don't they look like it ? But would Ferneley or Wolstenholme have dared ?

In 1812, Marshall moved from London to Newmarket. In 1820 he was badly smashed up in a coaching accident, from the effects of which he never recovered.

In 1825 he returned to London, where he died ten years later.

The sparkle was gone, the animated crowd acclaiming the winner had become a line of dots and dashes. The sun no longer shone. Towards the end he had to supplement his income by sporting journalism under the name of "Observator" in the *Sporting Magazine*, which had faithfully supported him for forty years.

Mrs. Macdonald-Buchanan of Cottesbrooke has a magnificent collection of both Marshall and Ferneley, probably the best in the world.

Ben Marshall had two famous pupils, John Ferneley, 1782-1860, and Abraham Cooper, 1787-1868. Cooper exhibited 332 pictures at the Royal Academy and contributed 262 to sporting magazines, but he never attempted a big hunting scene, nor is he in the same class as his master or his fellow pupil.

John Ferneley was the son of the Duke of Rutland's wheelwright and was born in the Hobey Vale. He was apprenticed for three years by the Duke to Marshall. Having served his time, he started his career in Ireland where he painted many pictures for Lord Lismore, which now hang at Burton-in-the-Wold within a few miles of the artist's birthplace, having been inherited by the late Earl of Huntingdon.

There will always be a disagreement as to whether master or pupil painted a horse best, though no one will disagree that Ben's portraits outshine John's as much as John's hunting pictures do Ben's. They remained close friends, however, and when Ferneley settled in Melton Mowbray in 1803 he never went to London without a Melton Pie or a small Stilton for his old master. He used to do studies of horses in Marshall's style for him to introduce into his pictures and I have seen Marshall's groups, where I have been almost certain of Ferneley's handiwork.

People are slow to recognise what lies under their very noses. For a hundred years half the big houses round Melton possessed a Ferneley Hunt Scurry.

They were scattered by retired Meltonions (ten seasons was a long innings) from Cadlands on the Solent to Keith Hall, Inverurie. Yet because they were cheap, £120 at most, no one recognised them as the great masterpieces of their kind. It took the Americans to wake us up to that fact and when the Wilton Scurry portraits by Grant sold for £2,400 by auction and

PTARMIGAN SHOOTING
Coloured engraving after Philip Reinagle, c. 1810

THOMAS TERTIUS PAGET, ESQ., M.P., AND HIS WIFE, GERALDINE McCAUSLAND,
ON 'SATAN' AND 'JESSICA' IN BRADGATE PARK
From the original oil painting by John Ferneley, senr., 1852

passed on at a good profit within a week to America, people began to sit up and take notice.

In a previous chapter I stated what are the requirements for a good sporting picture. Is one requirement missing here? Design, the orderly disorder. Can you fault it? Five men charging down abreast, every one with an individual seat. Compare Geary and Wilton's. The same applies to the Musgrave Scurry or the Massey Stanley. The landscapes, however simple, are typical of Leicestershire. The colourings soft and blended. But Ferneley besides being an artist was a hunting farmer. When staying with the great ones of the land, he is more interested in how his hay and horses are getting on without him than in the grand company. It will be noticed how fond he is of painting back views. They would probably be all he would see of the gods from his half-legged horse. He is best known for his ten guinea portraits of horses, C.O.D. He knew his Meltonians too well to give credit. I have eight of these portraits and each is a different type, from my grandmother's fat cob to her husband's slashing 17-hand weight-carrying thoroughbred, or the cross fired Leopard from the Quorn Stables to Ralph Lambton's short-tail brown hunter.

With the exception of the *Doings of Count Sandor* and one or two racehorses, very few of his pictures were engraved. Not a single one of his important hunting pictures had ever been reproduced before they appeared in *The Melton Mowbray of John Ferneley*, 1931.

Having started as a cart painter he knew how to mix and lay his paint to withstand the roughest usage. I have never seen a bad, cracked or faded picture by him, though I bought one a few years ago which had never been varnished! His *modus operandi* was to do separate pencil sketches of his subject and background, often several, transfer them on to a small experimental canvas, or combine them in a finished pencil drawing. The landscape grew with the subject. Finally he would get as many men and horses as would consent to give him a personal sitting. He enjoyed great popularity amongst the limited set who knew him; but, like his master, he "did'ner hold with that there Academy" and seldom tempted fortune. Yet at Osberston, the Durdans, Streely, Ashwardby and the Inch, a room, generally the dining room, is given up to his pictures alone. And no more suitable place "if your claret is very good and your port old."

Then can you and your son's son say:
> "Stand a tiptoe when this day is named
> And rouse him at the name of Vulpian;
> Then will he point and show his horse——
> Old men forget and all shall be forgot
> But he'll remember with advantages
> What feats he did that day.
> Then shall the names
> Edward the King, Wilton and Exeter,

Warwick and Talbot, Ashton Smith and Gloucester
Be in their flowing cups freshly remembered."

Eheu fugaces! It is much easier to ride a horse and cross a county with your knees under the mahogany and your toes in front of a fire than on a cold slippery saddle !

Ferneley died comparatively well off and left a large family. John junior, of York, 1815-1862, and Claude Lor(r)aine, 1822-1891, godson of C. Loraine Smith, were both good artists. John migrated to York and was much patronised by the officers at the Cavalry Barracks there. Sarah Ferneley engraved several of her father's pictures on stone, including *The Leopard* and *Samuel Dumbleton*, whipper-in to Dick Knight. John junior in many ways resembled his father but both subject and landscape are less fine and clear cut. He did a few Hunt Scurries but they are not important. Quite a lot of his work is attributed to his father, but on careful examination either "junior" or York is found; both brothers were most scrupulous about not attempting to palm their pictures off as their father's. When Claude helped the old man, it is recorded in the account book and a smaller price is charged. Claude was unfortunately lazy and unambitious, otherwise he would have gone far. He had a great sense of design and drew as well as his father. His water colours are excellent, well up to Henry Alken's when he took trouble. *The Meet at Kirby Gate*, 1856, is a good example. The horses in the foreground are easily identified as those his father painted for Thomas Paget about the same time.

David Dalby, 1790-1840, of York is an interesting study. Little is known of him except he lived round York in the first half of the nineteenth century. He was employed by the leading families of the county, especially those round Hurworth. Two of his racehorses, *Bran*, 1834, and *Mango*, 1837, appeared in the *Sporting Magazine*. He did cattle pictures but his best works are small hunting pictures. His paints have preserved their original brilliance and look like enamel on copper. He was a hunting man without a doubt, his horses' action is very life-like, his design is generally good. But alas, he took early to the bottle. The last we hear of him is that Mr. Booth of Killerby, the cattle breeder, and a few others guaranteed him twenty hunters to paint at the huge sum of £3 3s. each !

SPORTING PRINTS

THE PROCESS OF PRINTING

PRINTS are almost the only medium by which the general public can know anything of sporting art. They have enjoyed more popularity during the last two hundred years amongst all classes than any other school, not only in England but on the Continent.

PORTRAIT OF THE ARTIST, WITH TWO POINTERS
Sketch in oils by Ben Marshall, 1767-1835

I know of nothing that will brighten up a dark gloomy room more than a set of Pollard, Alken, Morland, Cooper-Henderson, Jones or Reinagle; racing, hunting, farming, coaching, fishing, shooting—to suit all tastes and all purses and most forms of interior decoration. They bring a breath of

23

fresh air into the room and they take us back to happy days or spur us on in the daily struggle with hopes of better things, when our ship comes home. Their artistic value varies as much as their price. A coloured mezzo-tint by Bell, Ward or Reynolds after Morland, in its first state, is as lovely as anything the artist has yet produced, while an aquatint by C. Hunt after F. C. Turner is very near the other extreme—£1,000 to 1s.

Space does not permit me to go deeply into the various ways in which prints are produced, but a very short note on their production may not be out of place. This should be easy for one, who for years has collected old prints and helped to produce new ones, but I soon found myself well out of my depth and so went back to school (Art), where printing is a speciality, and came out as wise as I went in. No-one could tell me *exactly* how Alken coloured his best aquatints, otherwise than by hand. They lent me an excellent book by Mr. Poortenaar of two hundred closely printed pages containing about 100,000 words, 90 illustrations and 43 specimens. It begins "This little book must be brief, but it could almost assume the size of the Encyclopaedia Britannica." Alas ! I must be briefer still !

There are woodcuts. There are mezzo, stipple and aquatints. There are dry point etchings and soft ground etchings, steel engravings and lithographs, all under the heading—Prints.

These processes cover all sporting prints up to about 1850. Then comes the camera and mass production. No man knows how many different and semi-demi-different processes of reproduction in colour there are to-day and if he did and wrote them down, he would probably be wrong to-morrow. But they have one thing in common. They are reproductions, not productions, their origin being the camera lens, while those enumerated above are the product of the artist's eye and the craftsman's hand. I do not wish to condemn them, many are as beautiful as the hand-made, but they are just reproductions.

Printing can be divided into three categories :
1. Relief Prints
2. Intaglio Prints
3. Plane or Lithograph Prints

The photographic processes group on the same principle :
1. Relief Prints—line and half tone.
2. Intaglio—heliogravure, flat plate, rotary—photogravure.
3. Planographic Prints—collotype, photo-litho, offset litho, Pantone, process, etc.

I can say no more about the mechanical printing processes which are improving every day. They range from Comic Cuts in two colours to a twelve or more colour half tone process; from thirty foot posters to postage stamps.

Woodcuts are the most ancient form of printing; dating from about A.D. 900, they, it is thought, came from China. Like many other inventions,

ESSEX HARRIERS

From the original oil painting by Dean Wolstenholme, senr, 1757–1837

PARTRIDGE SHOOTING

Stipple engraving by C. Catton after George Morland, 1763–1804

the printing press came into being in several places about the middle of the fifteenth century. In the earliest printed works whole words, pages and pictures were carved out of wood in reverse, the part to take the ink being in relief to receive the ink, the "whites" being "cut" away. This is the true woodcut and termed Relief Printing.

Next came wood engraving. Here the lines are cut or graved out of the wood, the ink forced into them and wiped off the smooth surface. Damp paper is then pressed on the block and sucks out the ink. The deeper the cut, the blacker the line. This is termed Intaglio Printing.

One form of this process is the mezzotint invented about 1642 by Ludwig von Siegen and Prince Rupert. Some say the Prince discovered this by idly rubbing pictures on the rust of a cannon and then sitting on his handkerchief, which he laid by chance over his "picture" to protect his breeches. On rising he found that an impression of his picture had adhered to the linen. Others say that he carried off a portrait of his lady love where such things are not generally displayed. Mezzo is the reverse to all other methods, which are worked from light to dark, while mezzo works from dark to light. That is to say, if you put a newly prepared mezzo plate through the press it would give a completely black surface, while the others would give a completely white one.

A mezzo plate is prepared by rocking or hatching, i.e., by making thousands of burrs all over the plate (generally copper) in every direction until it attains a uniform roughness. The design is then traced on this roughness, the lights being made by taking down the roughness, tones from pitch black to pure white being provided. They can be coloured in the same way as aquatints. Mezzo is by far the most beautiful and expensive printing process. It takes the engraver many months to finish a single plate and many hours to place the colours on it for each "pull." The smallest mishap may completely ruin a print. The engraver is an artist, not a workman. The number of good impressions from a copper plate are strictly limited, as it soon wears "flat." The most usual way of making pictures on metal plates is by graving or biting the lines into the surface of the plate by acid.

To produce a Dry Point a hard shellac varnish, called the ground, is painted over the plate and the picture scratched on it with an etching pen or stylus. In a Soft Ground Etching, instead of a shellac "ground" a soft tallowy mixture is used. The plate is then placed in an acid bath, until the metal surface exposed by the etched lines is bitten to the desired depth. For half tones or shading, lines and dots of varying depth and closeness are used.

Where no lines are used but only dots, even for the outline, it is called Stipple. Line engravings are produced on a similar principle, parallel lines being used in the same manner as dots. In a few cases the lines, as in wood engraving, are ploughed out of the metal by hand but this is very rare nowadays.

25

Plane or lithographs are produced generally from stones, but zinc is also used. The process is based on the antipathy of grease and water. One part of the stone's polished surface is drawn on with pen and special ink or greasy pencil. The paper being impressed on the stone picks up the ink from the treated portion, the untreated portion having rejected the ink from the rollers. The part which is required to be printed red, blue, yellow, etc., is treated on separate stones. These can be printed with or without an outline, and the outline printed either first or last according to the kind of ink used. Steel-etchings can also be coloured by this method and as many as twenty different colour printings may be carried out on one print. The disadvantage in this method is that there is no light and shade of colour, so the result tends to be "flat." Woodcuts are coloured in the same way, separate blocks being used for each colour.

Aquatints are produced much in the same way as Mezzo, but here the hatching is done by acid instead of by a rocker. The plate is dusted with powdered resin and then heated to form the ground. This leaves millions of tiny dots protecting the plate. The part required to be white is varnished over to protect it from the acid and the plate is then dipped for a few moments in the acid and parts unprotected by resin or varnish are slightly bitten, after which these lightest tones are protected and so on till dead black is obtained. The plate may then be worked up with a scraper to darken and a burnisher to lighten as with a mezzo tint. The "ground" can also be produced by dissolving the resin in pure alcohol and flooding the plate with it. It will be seen from these few words, how much success depends on the skill and experience of the plate-maker.

Colour printing is done by the printer first inking the plate all over with a dabber. The plate is then wiped with a series of canvas cloths. More ink is left on some parts than on others according to the discretion of the printer. The colours are painted on the plate by means of paper stamps and when all outlines have been filled in so as to produce a facsimile of the original picture, the plate is polished in the same way as with the foundation ink which was wiped off with a cloth and it is usually finished off with the palm of the printer's hand.

The plate now looks perfectly clean, but when passed through a high pressure press it will be found that enough ink has been left to give the required result. Usually as many as twenty different colours are used. Ink, paper, wiping and pressure of the press all affect the result. This pressure soon deteriorates the plate after about forty impressions. I am indebted to Messrs. Ackermann, the great producers of aquatints, for this information.

The Baxter Prints invented early in the 19th century are no longer made. They required a very great many hand-carved blocks for one picture, a separate block being required for each bit of colour. The majority of old sporting prints are termed aquatints and the only difference between many

HAWKING
Detail from a coloured engraving after Sawrey Gilpin and George Barett
by T. Morris, 1780

of them and watercolour drawings is that the former are painted over a
printed outline and the latter over a pencil outline.

The method by which prints of all kinds, hand-coloured included, were
produced was generally this—the artist drew his picture in oil or watercolour, then he or an etcher copied it on the plate from which the etcher
would take pulls or proofs until he got one to his and the artist's satisfaction.

This was then handed to the colourist, who copied it as near to the pattern as his ability enabled him, either by hand or other process. I possess a mezzo—*Ralph Lambton on Undertaker*, by Charles Turner after James Ward, R.A., marked in ink in the margin "Mr. Turner Pattern."

When a large set or a big issue of hand coloured prints was being produced many men were employed. This accounts for the inequality of merit often found in different sets and even in individual pictures of the same set. This also, to a lesser degree, applies to true aquatints.

The wages of a colourist could not have been high, for many books with forty-eight engravings were sold for one or two guineas. The panorama of a fox hunt eleven feet long and containing many hundreds of figures was published in a roll-up case at £1. 11s. 6d. If publishers, agents, papermakers, blockmakers and booksellers received the same proportion as they do to-day and the artist and author had taken their cut, not much meat would be left over for the colourist. What surprises me is, not that their efforts are so often poor, but that they are sometimes first class. In fact, if the colourists had only signed their work, we would find many names, which later became renowned. It was a way to earn bread, if not butter, while waiting for fame.

People often write and ask me the value of a set of prints. My reply is, I can no more value a print without seeing it and knowing its pedigree and condition, than I can a racehorse. One set of H. Alken, *Quorn Hunt*, has been sold for £1,200; and another for 48s. framed! I think the former the cheaper as it is as certain as anything can be that they were coloured by Alken himself; the latter being a modern pull from the old plates shockingly retouched and coloured by a "dustman."

In many cases it takes a magnifying glass to tell the first-rate print from the original watercolour. The earliest sporting water-colours I have seen are a set of four coursing ones by the elder Wolstenholme (1757-1837) engraved by Reeve in 1807. I bought them for a song 30 years ago in Northampton in very dirty frames and did not discover they were the original drawings until I took them out to clean.

The Wolstenholmes, father and son, used to colour their prints in oils themselves. This has caused the downfall of many a collector, professional as well as amateur, who thought he had secured an original set in bad condition, only to find them oil coloured prints, when he has started to restore them. I have met Morlands treated in the same way. Why oil prints are ranked so vastly inferior to aquatints I have never understood, and I only wish it had been my good fortune to come across a set of oil Wolstenholmes for sale. A West End dealer, who had fallen for one, refused point blank to sell it to me at any price.

This is only the very roughest idea of the many processes that exist and I am well aware that any expert can point to many omissions but I hope few serious errors.

PARTRIDGE SHOOTING
Oil painting by Samuel Alken, 1784-c.1825

THE MAKERS OF SPORTING PRINTS

FRANCIS BARLOW, of Lincolnshire, was one of the first engravers of sporting prints, but I have not come across any printed in colour, though hand-coloured specimens, some quite modern, are to be met with. Some he etched himself from his own pencil and indian ink drawings; the majority appeared in the *Gentleman's Recreation*, 1686. There are several prints after Wootton and Seymour but they were not published until after their deaths.

Stubbs and Marshalls are met with in colour, mezzo, stipple and aquatint but it was the Alkens and Wolstenholmes who did most to popularise sporting prints.

The Alkens stretch from Sefferin, a wood carver (1717-1782), by family tradition the son of a refugee who had fled from the court of Christian VII of Denmark where he had loved unwisely and too high, to his great grandson, Henry Gordon (H. Alken, junior) who died in 1894. One of the original Sefferin's sons, Samuel, was an architect and engraver and four of his sons, Sam, Henry, George and Sefferin were sporting artists, as in turn were two

BEATING SUGAR CANES FOR A HOG
Coloured aquatint after Samuel Howitt and Captain Williamson by Henry Merke
from *Field Sports of the East*, 1807

of Henry's, Henry (junior) and another Sefferin. Shaw Sparrow unravelled this tangled skein with his usual ability and industry in his *Book of Sporting Painters*.

As they all painted the same subject in the same style and signed their picture S. or H. Alken, it is impossible to tell by the signature alone, to which to attribute their work. The last Alken, christened Samuel Henry, called Henry Gordon, and signing his pictures H. Alken, junior, did his father's name much harm by not only omitting the "junior" but deliberately forging and passing off his very inferior work as that of his father. He died in the workhouse.

Henry Alken, senior, "Ben Tally Ho" (1785-1851) was the son of Samuel Alken (1756-1815), who had studied under J. T. Barber and became well known as a portrait painter; Henry started as a miniature painter. Christopher North in *Blackwood's* of 1824 describes H. Alken—"He is a gentleman and has lived with gentlemen. He understands their nature both in its strength and its weakness. . . . It is he that can escort you to Melton. . . . He feels the line that separates the true old *domine terrarum* and the *nouveau riche*. He feels this and paints as he feels." This disposes of the canard in *Notes and Queries*, that he started life as a valet and was a hunt servant at Badminton. The mystery about him is that for several seasons he mixed with the "nobs" at Melton as one of them, but none of them knew that he was "Ben Tally Ho," whose pictures they so admired, till he let it out at Kirby Gate during a dinner with that fiery radical politician and Tory fox hunter, Sir Francis Burdett. Where did he get enough money to start? Was it from horse coping? He wrote a treatise on that art. How many pictures did he paint and how many were engraved? I believe both G. Forbes and the late Mr. Schwert tried to compile a complete list, but gave it up, when they got near five figures!

No phase of life came amiss to him. He could turn over a gig, knock down a pheasant or a Charlie, gallop over a brook or a snob, caricature the ridiculous uniforms of the Prince Regent's Army and even Prinny himself, but certainly not "The Duke." *The Man whom Boney could not turn* is full of dignity. His Hunt Scurrys, though too bunched up and crowded, move. He is too fond of one class of horse, not because he could not draw a screw as well as Leech, but because he liked that class. His colouring is clear and vivid without being crude, his lines are like his fun, clean and sharp. When he sat down to paint a picture, his composition is as good as anyone's. It is only, when carried away by the pace of the hunt, that he forgets such trifles.

COURSING
Coloured aquatint after Philip Reinagle by Nichols and Black, 1815

31

His landscapes are as good as Birkett Foster's. His atmosphere is transparent, his snow sparkles. I don't always like his hounds' shoulder action, nor is his arrangement of his field up to Ferneley's best—not so natural. Lady Daresbury's collection contains some masterpieces. His oils fall off sadly in comparison with his watercolours; the drawing is there and the spirit, but not the purity of colour. He loses distance. But, when judging them, remember that other members of the family undoubtedly did the worst and put "H. Alken" on them, though these could not deceive anyone who wasn't blind. I would rather have the first rate print than the original oil painting. Why will watercolour artists try and do oils?

Amongst other activities he used to "engrave" the amateur efforts of his sporting friends. In most cases "engrave" was a euphemism for completely redrawing and colouring the originals in his own style. I have seen the originals for the *Beaufort Hunt* by W. P. Hodges at the late Sir Julian Cahn's.

They differ from Alken's engravings as chalk from cheese; in fact he cut some in half and made two prints out of one. Those he engraved for Sir R. Frankland and Mr. Dean Paul also show the master hand. He redrew *Dick Knight's Doings* for Loraine Smith, but the tough old squire would have none of them, preferring his own crudities and cursing Jukes, the engraver, for improving them.

Alken never left his mother lodge, even when drawing a large crowd: he was always a miniaturist. Many of his fancy pictures are a collection of miniatures of real horses and men. In fact, I doubt whether he could avoid doing this, if he had tried.

Many of his best works he etched direct on to the plates and coloured them himself. Some must have been done from small sketches. My reason for saying this is that so few of the originals of his prints are extant. What remain to us prove that his original drawings would never have been destroyed if they had ever existed. Spencer of Oxford Street, a great admirer of H. Alken, found the pencil drawings, quarter size, of the *Quorn Hunt*, but no one claims to own the "originals," though I believe Lord Haddington's set of prints to have been coloured by Alken himself.

The Pollards come next in popularity. Robert was born in 1756 and died in 1838, and James his son was born in 1772, dying in 1867. They were both of the Alken School, but their draftsmanship was very inferior. Their horses' legs are far too long and thin. They excelled in racing, coursing, coaching and fishing pictures, but their hunting pictures are very inferior. They were obviously not hunting men. History is deep in their debt for the detail in their prints of our race courses and coursing meetings. Mr. Gilbey has a fine selection of the originals of their fishing prints, which are very pleasing. Neither were great artists but both were good illustrators. Their backgrounds are very true to life and easily recognised by those who know the localities from which they were taken.

By courtesy of Captain and the Hon. Mrs. Macdonald-Buchanan

POINTERS

From the original oil painting by Sir Edwin Landseer, R.A., 1802-1873

A MEET OF THE QUORN AT KIRBY GATE
From the original water colour by Claude Loraine Ferneley, 1859

Squire Loraine Smith of Enderby, the Maecenas of sporting artists, was largely a caricaturist. He might have been a great artist, if he had ever been taught to draw and paint, for he had that subtle instinct for design. In prints made after his drawings his animals are anatomically incorrect, but they are very much alive and when Alken redrew the Squire's *Dick Knight* he lost some of the truth and vigour. He alone has the honour of sharing a plate with Morland, *A litter of Foxes, animals by Charles Loraine Smith, Esq., landscape by George Morland; engraved by Grozer.*

The squire provided Morland with an open hearth at Enderby when his creditors were too hot on his scent, and it was during his stays in Leicestershire, that he produced some of his best work. The story goes that the squire took the cellar key with him when he went out hunting. One day on his return he looked at one of his own pictures which he had left unfinished. "Best thing I've ever done," he exclaimed, "a bottle of port is indicated, eh, my boy!" George agreed and saw to it that the squire was equally pleased on his next return.

Morland could not draw a hound to save his life. In the hunting set by Bell "the dogs" are quite different in each picture and not fox hounds of any known breed in one of the four, but that does not stop them being superb pictures, colour, design, composition—perfect. A good set is worth £1,000.

It is with mezzotints we associate Morland, and there are no finer prints in the world; many of these are engraved by his brothers-in-law, J. R. Smith and William Ward. J. M. W. Turner, Rowlandson, Sam Howitt and several more who became artists of repute helped to produce J. R. Smith's mezzotints, not only from the works of sporting artists such as Chalon and Ben Marshall, but from those of Sir Joshua Reynolds, Opie and a host more.

Samuel Howitt's forty aquatints for Thomas Williamson's *Oriental Sports* must not be left out. They are a remarkable achievement for a man who had never seen India. A book of his *Twenty British Field Sports* fetched £1,060 in New York in 1923. But there is too much sameness about Howitt's horses. They are all half-bred Arabs and his hunting scenes, though well painted, tend to be too pretty. They fail to carry conviction. He somehow lacks guts.

I have already alluded to the Wolstenholmes—father 1757-1837, and son 1798-1883. They were originally Yorkshire squires, who came south to Essex to hunt over a property there, but strayed into that dangerous, tricky country round Chancery Court, where they lost and were ruined. They, however, made their second horse serve as their first. Instead of hunting to paint, they painted to hunt, so for once some good came out of Chancery. They both painted equally well in oils and water-colours. Their knowledge of hunting is accurate and delicate. They would have been better known if they had migrated to Melton, but they preferred the southern counties of Essex, Hertfordshire and Surrey. The majority of their pictures are small, few being over two feet by eighteen inches and many a quarter of that size.

They reproduce exceedingly well, so well in fact, that a few years ago the market was flooded with cheap forgeries. Up to 1817, Reeve of Grafton Street engraved most of the father's work, when his son undertook the job. All I have come across are aquatints. As both signed their pictures Dean Wolstenholme, the father's and son's works are hard to distinguish.

Amongst other artists, who made sporting prints, R. B. Davis (1783-1854), son and brother of Royal Huntsmen, enjoyed great popularity and deserved it. Though his fox and hounds tend to be too big in proportion to his horses, no one sits his man better down in his saddle. Many of his prints are lithographs, which are apt to be flat, but the mezzo by Wagstaff of *John Musters and His Hounds* is very fine. His Majesty the King has many good specimens of his work at Windsor.

H. B. Chalon (1771-1849) was also much patronised by royalty. He was of foreign extraction and did most of his work in the North, where coal, up to the present, has enabled his patrons' descendants to hang on to his work, so that very few have found their way into the market. There are several good mezzos by W. Ward after him.

Commander Bower's *Sir Mark Sykes and His Hounds* is a grand hunting picture, full of truth and vigour. It is well known through the first class mezzo by William Ward. Lord Barnard's *The Raby Pack*, which is sometimes met in colour, is equally good.

Cooper-Henderson (1803-1877), born with the rise of the mail coach, saw its zenith and died with its extinction. No man ever made the dust fly, chains

GOING TO THE FAIR
Oil painting by J. F. Herring, sen., 1841

34

A STEEPLECHASE
Oil painting by John Dalby, 1853

rattle and lanterns gleam as he does. *The Windsor Coach at Full Speed* and *Returning from Ascot Races* must always keep their places as long as any remain who cherish memories of The Road before it became a tarred skating rink.

He has been well served by his engraver, J. Harris; his horses live. He is far better than Pollard. There is no real comparison, but there is no-one else to compare him to! If he has a fault, it is that he is inclined to over-emphasise unnecessary details in the foreground and his effect is often too shiny. Maggs, during the later part of the last century copied Cooper Henderson's style and produced some splendid "old" coaching scenes, but they somehow just miss the sparkling truth of Cooper-Henderson.

The Herrings, F. C. Turner and Harry Hall did much to kill sporting prints.

They produced too much and too many were very poor stuff. Most of them are stencil portraits of racehorses which grateful backers bought to remind themselves they had once backed a winner. No ale-house was complete without them.

Herring senior started life as a stage-coach driver and painter. If he had been taught drawing instead of driving and painting pictures instead of carriages, he would have gone far. He undoubtedly had great natural genius; his farmyard scenes are full of understanding and feeling, but are often too busy. His racing pictures show knowledge and strength, but when he tries something big, he falls down, as he does, when he attempts hunting scenes. One sickens of his two carriage horses and the Sultan's white Arab, which Queen Victoria gave him, jumping stiffly on hounds; yet he was the most popular sporting painter of the day.

35

Both F. C. Turner, Hunt and Hall's hunting pictures are beneath contempt. Unlike Morland, their lack of truth is not redeemed by artistic merit. Neither artist was happy in his engraver. Both were born in the machine age and were swept along with it.

Lastly there comes Sir Edwin Landseer. No artist ever enjoyed such popularity or, during his life, such high prices. Fifty years ago "proof" steel engravings after him, fetched hundreds and a very insignificant original a thousand pounds. A portrait of three hunters was valued in 1902 at £8,000 for probate and the engravings from the private plate at £120 each. To-day you could knock off a nought and call it shillings! Yet Landseer is a great artist. He was untrue to his genius. He glutted an adoring public with poorer and poorer, stickier and stickier sentimentality, highly polished. He played down to the crowd like a bad comedian, till they gave him the "bird" for giving them what they asked for. Fortunately for him he had been dead fifty years, leaving £200,000, before his public tired of him.

With the death of Henry Alken, sporting prints rapidly deteriorated and lost much of their popularity. The photograph was creeping in and in its wake cheap and gaudy colour processes which murdered the delicacy of Alken and Wolstenholme. Not until after Queen Victoria died did photographic reproduction attain anything like success. To-day, water-colours can be very well reproduced, but the finest modern process printing is by no means easy or cheap.

The nineteenth century illustrators must not be forgotten. First of these is John Leech (1817-1864), the creator of Jorrocks and Mr. Briggs. Then there was his successor on *Punch*, Charles Keene (1823-1891). Randolph Caldecott (1846-1886) was one of the same school, the delight of the nursery; he might have risen to great things, if he had lived longer and ever enjoyed good health. He could draw and his colour was pure and natural. Sporting illustrators deteriorated far less than the painters. Finch Mason, Armour, Beer, the Tout, Snaffles and the Wag are worthy successors of Leech. Though not mentioned in most books on the Water-colour School, the men touched on here are up to the best standard and contributed much to popularise water-colours. Edward Duncan (1804-1882) was a link between the two Schools.

Duncan etched John Ferneley's *Doings of Count Sandor*, as well as other pictures for sporting artists and was a leading light amongst the many fine water-colourists in the first half of the last century.

Lionel Edwards and Charles Simpson are artists of the first rank. Besides having had many of their works reproduced in colour, they have illustrated their own and other people's books. Simpson, in connection with Messrs. Gee of Leicester, produced by a new process chalk drawings almost indistinguishable from the originals. But I do not think that the new processes, or the new men, will ever entirely out the old.

CHILLINGHAM WILD BULL
Wood engraving by Thomas Bewick, 1789

BEGINNING OF PICTORIAL ADVERTISING

THAT Britain breeds the best horses, cattle and sheep is denied by no-one who has studied the subject. For years they have been exported to every corner of the world. It is equally true that they deteriorate in foreign climates unless reinforced by home-grown stock every few generations.

This is most peculiar in the case of our racehorses, which are 90 per cent. pure Arab. They remain superior to their desert-bred brethren in every respect, except soundness. It is the same with foreign breeds of dogs, such as Spanish Pointers, St. Bernards, Pomeranians, Golden Russian Retrievers, Alsatians, which permanently improve in this country. Many show winners, bred here for several generations, return to the land of their origin to improve the native stock. But shows have undoubtedly spoilt the usefulness of many breeds by exaggerating certain points, and the artists have helped to do the same.

The horse has come off best in Art. His eye might be too big and his head too small, or his legs too thin, but the worst looked something like a

37

horse. It is no good exaggerating a racehorse too much. Even in 1700 there was a racing calendar and the racecourse to prove a horse's mettle. In the eighteenth century, travel was not only expensive and uncomfortable but, in winter, well-nigh impossible. In 1797, shows had hardly been organised. The Agricultural Society was not "Royal" when it commissioned James Ward to do a picture of every breed of cattle and sheep in England. There was no other way to compare their merits. When he had done over two hundred the project failed and Ward said he lost hundreds, but what he lost on the swings, he amply made up on the roundabouts in the form of friends and patrons amongst the highest in the land.

Arthur Young (1741-1820) tells us that, in 1810, "a very alert agrarian pride gave pleasure also to many lawyers, physicians, soldiers, sailors, wealthy merchants. Farming is made up from all ranks from a duke to an apprentice. There have been more experiments and more discoveries and more general good sense displayed within these ten years than in the hundred preceding them."

But long before 1810, there had been a wave of experiments all over England, which, starting with a horse, went on to all sorts of farm animals. Since 1650, war had definitely ceased to be the occupation of gentlemen; it was the affair of the Government and their "damned scum of a standing army." To work off their energy, they devoted themselves to farm improvement, not only in breeding but also in winter feeding and the production of feeding stuffs.

These experimenters wanted a shop window. Who the wealthy merchant was, who first harnessed Art to the Cattle Trade, I do not know. There is no record of any breeder being impeached for pictorial exaggeration. These merchants employed the best artists of the day, and had their pictures engraved in mezzo and stipple as well as line, sparing no expense. Barlow painted an ox of 19 hands high and 3 ft. 6 ins. across the hips. Of them all, Robert Bakewell (1725-1795) of Dishley, Leicestershire, was the most famous improver of cattle and sheep, though to Thomas Bates (1775-1849) belongs the credit of the modern Shorthorn dairy cattle produced by methods of intense inbreeding. Bakewell was indeed the high priest of this new cult, and the highest in the land flocked to Dishley, leaving with pedigree bulls and rams purchased at fancy prices.

The animal portrait painter's life was not all plain sailing. Thomas Bewick (1753-1828), the wood-engraver and naturalist of Newcastle, has left behind him an account of his experiences at Barmpton, as Sparrow tells us in *Walker's Quarterly* :

"After I had made my drawings from the fat sheep, I soon saw that they were not approved, but that they were to be made like certain paintings shown to me. I observed to my employer that the paintings bore no resemblance to the animals whose figures I had made my drawings from; and that I would not alter mine to suit the paintings that were shown to me; but, if

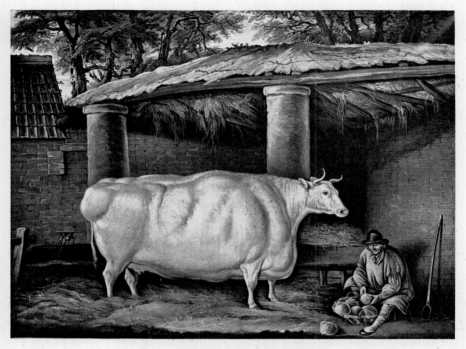

COLLING'S WHITE SHORTHORN HEIFER
Mezzotint after Thomas Weaver by William Ward, 1811

it were wished that I should make engravings from these paintings, I had not the slightest objection to do so, and I would also endeavour to make *facsimiles* of them. . . .

"This proposal would not do; and my journey as far as concerned these fat cattle makers ended in nothing. I objected to put lumps of fat here and there where I could not see it, at least not in so exaggerated a way as on the paintings before me; so ' I got my labour for my trouble.' "

.So much for his human friends; now for his bovine ones.

"With an old friend I went to Chillingham park where a splendid bull wheeled about and then confronted us. The creature became so threatening a hasty retreat was necessary. I was, therefore, obliged to endeavour to see one, which had been conquered by a rival and driven to seek shelter alone in the quarry hole or wood and in order to get a good look at one of this description I was under the necessity of creeping on hands and knees to leeward, out of sight and thus I got my sketch."

I wonder what Stubbs would have done? He tackled one of Lord Rockingham's stallions which broke away and attacked its portrait.

George Stubbs and Thomas Weaver dealt with tempers in a more subtle manner. They obeyed their patrons blindly. Look at *Colling's Heifer*. Was there ever such a monstrosity on sheep's legs? Note the smile of the man cutting turnips, the size of cannon balls, which are rolling out of the picture. Now turnips had only just been introduced into England by Dutch William, and were about the size of one's fist. Look at the *Lincolnshire Ox* turning a contemptuous back on Mr. Gibbons, while the game cock takes him off exactly. And this is by the same man who painted *Bulls Fighting !*

John Ferneley fared no better than Bewick, preferring his art to his pocket, so did very few cattle pictures but produced no monstrosities. Nor have I seen any palpable freaks by Ben Marshall. In his picture of *Mr. Wilkinson of Lenton's bull*, '*Alexander*,' he has left it with a very cowlike head and his pictures for Robert Bakewell of Dishley are true to life. Compare them with Garrard's *Holderness Cow*, 1798, and Thomas Weaver's *Bull Patriot*, 1810. Such animals could not have stood, let alone walk. Sparrow terms Weaver a follower of Stubbs. True, he makes a fool of his patron, as Stubbs does of Collins, and has almost copied Stubbs' labourer, but he followed the master too far behind to catch even his sarcasm.

Perhaps Boultbee exaggerates the length of my forbear's Longhorns but I hope not their beauty ! Anyway, they are "human cows" and took a cup at Smithfield the year before he died, 1811. George III may not have been a great Empire-maker, but he was no mean judge of a cow or a picture and he assigned Boultbee a house near Cumberland Lodge, from whence he could immortalise the royal stock.

What Bakewell was to breeding James Ward (1769-1859) was to painting cattle. He started as an apprentice to John Raphael Smith, the engraver, and was later appointed engraver to the Prince of Wales. He worked for Opie, Reynolds and Marshall, but he wanted to create on his own and not be a mere copyist. They implored him to continue with his engraving. George III asked him why he gave up a lucrative trade for so precarious a living as painting. "Sire, I engrave for my living, I paint for my pleasure." Some of his early work is very like Morland's but he was furious on hearing himself described as the pupil of his young brother-in-law. Cattle did not content him. He wanted to outshine Ben Marshall at racehorses. Egged on by Benjamin West, he competed with Paul Potter, who was then in vogue, and produced a group of *Mr. Allnutt's Aldency Cattle* (12 ft. x 18 ft.) now in the National Gallery; and with the great Rubens, when he hung his *Bulls Fighting Across a Tree at St. Donatt Castle* next to Rubens' *Chateau de Steen* in West's Studio.

There is a great manliness and vigour about Ward, which inspires trust. No man has ever painted old horses better. He is one of the few animal painters who have ever been favoured by the Royal Academy and exhibited 287 pictures there. Sir Edwin Landseer occasionally did stud animals, notably a British boar for Mr. Weston, M.P., in 1818, but he cannot be

By courtesy of the Artist and Captain and the Hon. Mrs. Macdonald-Buchanan

WINDSOR GREYS AT ASCOT
From the original oil painting by A. J. Munnings, P.R.A.

compared to Stubbs, Morland, Marshall, Henry Alken or Ferneley. Abraham Cooper (1787-1868) was another sporting and cattle painter, favoured by the R.A. He was elected in 1820 over the head of his master, Ben Marshall, his superior in every way, except that he was a friend of the Wards and a Londoner.

George Morland did many country scenes and kept a perfect menagerie at his house in London. He once rescued a sucking pig from an untimely oven and carried it squealing under his arm to visit a friend. To my knowledge, Morland never entered the "advertisement racket" during his life. Heaven help the man who would appeal to him for flattery. He wanted it all for himself. Yet, to-day, his pictures are used more than any other man's, to advertise scent, soaps, guns, whisky, hats, sweets, almost anything. Morland serves a great purpose. He brings us down to earth, the country earth of simple folk. His pigs are measly, his horses worn out and common, his cows tubercular, and his countrymen often dirty. He shows us the English stock before Bakewell and Collins reformed it.

Amongst the well-known sporting artists who painted cattle are the Wolstenholmes, Chalon, R. B. Davis and his brother, William. The Marquis of Exeter has a whole book of cattle studies by William Davis, who did a great many of his pictures up and down the country, which are often mistaken for his brother's, R. B. Davis's.

With so much wealth and talent at their disposal it is a pity the Royal Agricultural Society does not arrange an exhibition of cattle pictures. A single ox or pig may not be of much interest, but a comprehensive exhibition, where comparison is possible would be. If they only traced all they could of James Ward's two hundred, they could not fail to arouse attention and controversy. There are few country houses where the family have been rooted for two hundred years which do not boast at least one monstrosity of an ox. The only man who has ever done anything in this direction is Mr. Augustus Walker of the Walker Galleries, Bond Street. He has taken a lifelong interest in the subject. In 1930 and 1932 he staged two most interesting exhibitions, as ambitious as his comparatively small galleries would allow. They proved a great success, and both should have been acquired lock, stock and barrel for the nation by the Royal Agricultural Society or some other body.

Walter Shaw Sparrow wrote an excellent article in *Walker's Quarterly*, No. 33, which is as interesting to the farmer as it is to the collector. He gives some interesting figures of the cost of Mr. John Gibbons' *Lincolnshire Ox*, 1790, 26½ x 38½. Stubbs received £64 12s. 6d. (£20 on March 5th and £44 12s. 6d. on April 9th). G. T. Stubbs received £105 for engraving it (August 2nd and February 3rd); the engraver of the title, £1 11s. 6d.; Joe Stewardson of Grafton Street £15 15s. for printing 500 copies. In all £186 19s. On the top of this was the expense of bringing the ox from Long Sutton and a long stay in London. Though this seems, even to-day, a lot of money we must remember that prices of cattle ran high, too. Mr. Lawrence gave my ancestor £400 for the longhorn bull "Shakespeare" at the age of 17, and Mr. Fowler's herd of 53 fetched £4,289, "Brindled Beauty" £273; an average of £90 per head, and money worth four or five times what it is to-day.

The pictures I liked best at Walker's exhibitions were a couple of cattle fairs by J. Ferneley, *Birthday, of Castle Howard* by D. Dalby, a brilliant bit of white on black, and *Mr. Donald Cross's Ayrshire Cattle*, 1893, by Joseph Adam, R.S.A., which combines a fine free lowland landscape and four cows without senseless exaggeration.

Boultbee and his pupil, T. Weaver of Shrewsbury, were well represented as was Garrard by his fine scenes, *Whitbread's Brewery;* mezzotints by William Ward. There were four or five of *Leicester Long Wools* by T. Yeoman of Grantham, an artist I had not met before. Munning's Friesian bull, *Ongar Vic Klaas*, ought to have been there.

On coming away one could not help feeling, however, that such exhibitions are of more interest to the historian and the breeder than to the artist and connoisseur.

GAMES AND PASTIMES

MY definition of sports and games is that, in the former, man set his wit and strength against nature with or without the assistance of animals. Games are where man contends with man in friendly rivalry to demonstrate his superiority in some particular form of strength or skill. So far I have only touched on the sports, but there are many games and contests which are generally included under the heading "Sports." In fact it is very hard to know where to draw the line between the two. Coursing is undoubtedly a sport if carried out in order primarily to catch a hare, but a contest, if to test the relative speed of greyhounds. Racing though commonly regarded as a sport is in the true meaning of the word no such thing, but a cross between a contest, an entertainment and a business. The same can be said of league football and cricket. The mail coaches of Pollard and Cooper-Henderson are always regarded as sporting pictures but there is no more sport or pastimes about them than there is about a railway train. But the English are an illogical race who do not trouble about exact definitions and will always compromise over anything except about having no sense of humour or a bad seat on a horse. Trap-shooting at clay birds certainly does not come under sport any more than darts, but where is the difference between hand-reared pheasants out of wire netting enclosures and pigeons out of traps? Fortunately this is not the place to decide this knotty point. It is to Barlow we look for sport of the seventeenth century and to the Alkens and Rowlandson for sport and pastimes in the eighteenth and nineteenth. They did not attempt to differentiate between the two.

THE MAIL COACH AT THE ANGEL, ISLINGTON, ON THE NIGHT OF HIS MAJESTY'S BIRTHDAY
Coloured aquatint by James Pollard, 1812

Thomas Rowlandson, 1756-1827, a real cockney bred and born, shows with his chalks and washes every side of life with irrepressible fun and high spirits, not always restrained within the highest bounds of refinement and propriety. He was a fast worker and his original drawings are still to be picked up for a song out of old portfolios. His illustrations for *A Tour of Dr. Syntax* are very fine examples of eighteenth-century aquatints and show up the twentieth-century edition process plates very badly. Rowlandson has done some very fine landscapes but it is the fun and pace he put into his pictures that put him in the front rank.

Not till I started looking for illustrations for this book did I realise the paucity of pictures of our pastimes, not only of artistic merit but even of mere illustrations. Take the five most popular games in this country: football, cricket, golf, tennis and bowls. I do not know a single really good picture of one of them except possibly of cricket or of golf in some of the eighteenth-century Dutch school.

Yet golf should lend itself to "landscape figures" as much as fishing. Shaw Sparrow names several hundred men who have painted fishing pictures, but go into any golfer's home and how many golfing pictures do you find? One or two prints, perhaps, tucked away in the hall or passage or possibly in his den, but never in the principal rooms. The best known

43

PERCH FISHING
Oil painting by William Jones c. 1830

pictures of bowls are various modern versions of Sir Francis Drake where costume overweighs sport. The centre court at Wimbledon ought, with its light and shade, its greens and whites, to provide a motive to some rising Segar or Teniers. The late Jeremiah Colman had a great collection of cricket pictures, some of artistic value and interest, but most of just interest, though in the best of these there are fine landscape backgrounds.

Alas, the most common form of modern cricket picture is a collection of photographic heads stuck on unnatural bodies crowded inartistically together in front of an early Victorian pavilion with gas works or worse as a background. Ranji's *Jubilee Book* of cricket was entirely illustrated with photographs. Hundreds paint gardens and cottages, heaths and churches, the play of light through trees, but how many the village cricket match, combining all or some of these elements? Boxing and boxers attracted several artists, among them Ben Marshall, Rowlandson, H. Alken and Gilray.

On the Continent bull fighting has inspired artists of every school and posters advertising these shows often are magnificent both in colour and drawing, but I have never yet seen an inspiring advertisement inviting me to a Championship Fight or a League Football Final. The efforts made in this direction either for horse or dog racing are too feeble to mention.

Beer, Beef and Baccy have done far more for art than our organised games. The average Briton will thank his gods that there is no bull fighting in this enlightened country but little more than a hundred years ago, in every

44

town in England there was bull and bear baiting (bull baiting was enforced by law for hygienic reasons, for it was held by the medical profession that bull-flesh was rendered more wholesome if killed immediately after being baited), pigeon and sparrow shooting from traps, badger drawing, dog fighting and cock fighting; and any of the last four can still be enjoyed in some parts of the country.

At the 1942 Preston Exhibition of Sporting Pictures, one artist attempted to portray football, billiards and bowls by the modernist method. The results were not a success and aroused as much adverse comment both from the highbrow as from the vulgar. This, however, should not deter others trying. From a sportsman's or an artist's point of view both the camera and "the movie" have failed to reproduce games satisfactorily. "The Dogs" have fired a number of artists as did motor racing when it first started. Some Frenchmen produced pictures which gave the idea of speed and humour but one must be a motor salesman to see real beauty in a racing motorist or his car. Flying, too, has yet to produce its Stubbs or Leech.

Of the many artists who have tried their hand at Polo, Gilbert Holiday was probably the most successful. He was a master in depicting speed— no-one better—but his technique and knowledge just failed to put him in the top class. He died young, just before the 1939 war, from a fall with the Woolwich Drag on the top of wounds received twenty years earlier with the gunners.

THE REVIVAL OF SPORTING ART

FROM the beginning of the nineteenth century sporting art began to sink and by 1850 few of the old landmarks remained and no new ones had sprung up. The cause was two-fold : steam and the camera. Steam transformed the art patron from the landed magnate, rich in tradition and Napoleonic war profits, into the hard manufacturing materialist who looked on hunting as a dangerous waste of time and the horse as a slow means of locomotion. The camera cheapened portraiture. The sporting artist might have stood up to its competition if he had refused its help. By slavish use of it he proceeded to produce mere coloured photographs instead of original pictures; suspended motion, instead of the appearance of motion as recorded by the slower human eye.

The present century saw a great revival in animal painting in which many women took part, notably Lucy Kemp Welsh, Maud Earl, and such men as Wardell and Britton Rivière. But sporting pictures proper were still in disgrace. J. D. Giles struck out a line on his own, breaking the Alken tradition. He placed hunting scenes on well drawn natural backgrounds of nearly every hunt in England; the subject being subservient to the background. They are too photographic and his colouring too muddy to be great works of art but it was a stride forward.

The first phase of this war, 1914-1918, undoubtedly knocked out a generation of rising Alkens and Marshalls. Since the second phase started many well-known artists have dropped out, Lynwood Palmer, Ivester Lloyd, George Wright, Lucas Lucas, Cecil Aldin, George Talmadge and Gilbert Holiday; not giants perhaps, but head and shoulders above their fathers and most of the contemporary R.A.'s. The leaders of to-day are no way behind their eighteenth century forbears. Sir Alfred Munnings is the first animal painter to fill the high office of President of the Royal Academy. Munnings is a master of colour and the play of light and shade. Many of his admirers prefer his "rough" work, often dashed off while his "finished" pictures are drying. His *Pytchley Hounds Feeding* (1944 R.A.) attracted far more praise than his other pictures of that year. His Friesian bull, a study in greens, is a masterpiece equal to Rubens', Paul Potter's or Ward's best and his studies of the Belvoir Hounds in the snow though impressionistic in style, please both critic and sportsman.

Charles Simpson is undoubtedly the best bird painter living. He alone, of all artists past and present, can make his birds appear out of their backgrounds as one approaches them or the light is increased as in nature. But they require large canvasses and do not reproduce well, even by the most expensive processes. He is a great draughtsman and has done many first rate equestrian portraits.

Lionel Edwards, the other outstanding sporting artist, is a landscape painter in the very top class worthy to rank with any of the nineteenth century. He can paint a Hunt Scurry as good and life-like as Ferneley, on a background worthy of Birket Foster. His figures are as good or better portraits than Henry Alken's and have as much life and movement. No man softens his outlines with mist as he does and at the same time retains their truth and weight. He has only to see a hunt gallop once across his landscape to produce a dozen recognisable portraits of the men and their hunters.

We can only hope that men like Michael Lyne, Seago, Meade King, Peter Scott and many I have not yet met, may get through this war to carry on the traditions of their art.

Though Mr. Walter Hutchinson has not got very far with his National Gallery of Sports and Pastimes he has started to place the English Sporting School on a par with other Schools and to give both ancient and modern a fair run. With our new P.R.A., to teach portrait painting; Sanderson Wells and Lionel Edwards, hunting and shooting scenes; Charles Simpson and Peter Scott, birds; and Armour and Snaffles the fun of it; with Doris Crome Johnson to show that advanced modern technique handled with sense and discretion can be a suitable medium, the budding sporting painters will not lack leaders.

There is always room in front. "Too much," we old uns may sigh, but don't let that stop anyone. "See what is the other side of that hill in front." "Gang forrard! Gang forrard."

46

THE FLYE AT THE HAERON
Woodcut from *The Book of Falconrie and Hawking* by George Turberville, 1611

CHRONOLOGICAL LIST
OF THE PRINCIPAL BRITISH SPORTING ARTISTS

Francis Barlow	..	*c.*1626-1704	Robert Pollard ..	1756-1838
John Wootton	..	*c.*1686-1765	Dean Wolstenholme, sen.	1757-1837
Peter Tillemans	..	1684-1734	Julius Caesar Ibbetson	1759-1817
John Sartorius	..	1700-1779	J. N. Sartorius, jun. ...	1759-*c.*1825
James Seymour	..	1702-1752	George Garrard, A.R.A.	1760-1826
George Stubbs	..	1724-1806	George Morland ..	1763-1804
Sawrey Gilpin, R.A...		1733-1807	Charles Towne ..	1763-1840
Francis Sartorius	..	1735-1804	Samuel Howitt ..	*c.*1765-1822
Philip Reinagle, R.A.		1749-1833	Ben Marshall ..	1767-1835
Thomas Gooch	..	1750-1802	William Ward, A.R.A.	1768-1826
Charles Loraine Smith		1751-1835	James Ward, R.A. ..	1769-1859
John Raphael Smith		1752-1812	Henry Barnard Chalon	1771-1849
John Boultbee	..	1753-1812	James Pollard ..	1772-1867
Thomas Bewick	..	1753-1828	Clifton Tomson ..	*b.*1775
Samuel Alken	..	1756-1815	R. R. Reinagle, R.A...	1775-1862
Thomas Rowlandson		1756-1827	Thomas Weaver ..	1775-1844

James Barenger	1780-1831	Sir Francis Grant, P.R.A.	1803-1878
John Ferneley, sen.	1782-1860	William Barraud	1810-1850
Richard Barrett Davis	1783-1854	Samuel Henry Alken, jun.	1810-1894
Samuel Alken, jun.	1784-c.1825	Henry Barraud	1811-1874
Henry Thomas Alken, sen.	1785-1851	Richard Ansdell, R.A.	1815-1885
Abraham Cooper, R.A.	1787-1868	J. Ferneley, jun. (York)	1815-1862
David Dalby	1790-1840	H. K. Browne (Phiz)	1816-1882
F. C. Turner	1795-1846	John Leech	1817-1864
John Frederick Herring	1795-1865	Claude Loraine Ferneley	1822-1891
John Francis Sartorius *fl.*	1797-1831	Charles Keene	1823-1891
Dean Wolstenholme, jun.	1798-1883	Randolph Caldecott	1846-1886
Thomas Woodward	1801-1852	Lionel Edwards, R.I.	*b.*1878
George Henry Laport	1802-1873	Sir Alfred Munnings, P.R.A.	*b.*1878
Sir Edwin Landseer, R.A.	1802-1873	Lynwood Palmer	*d.*1939
Cooper Henderson	1803-1877	Charles Simpson, R.I.	*b.*1885

SHORT BIBLIOGRAPHY

The Gentleman's Recreation 1686.—*Animal Painters of England* by Sir W. Gilby, Bt., 1900.—*British Sporting Artists* 1922, *Angling in British Art* 1923 and *A Book of Sporting Painters* 1931 by Walter Shaw Sparrow.—*Sport in Art* by W. Baillie Grohman 1919.—*Sporting Prints* by Frank Siltzer.—*Melton Mowbray of John Ferneley* by Guy Paget 1931.—*Old Sporting Books* 1921 and *Sporting Prints* by Nevill.—*Walker's Magazine*

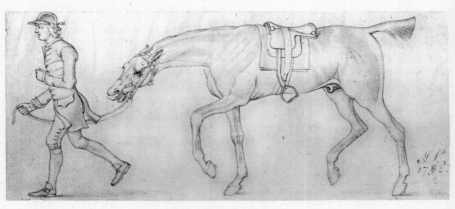

HORSE AND JOCKEY
Pencil drawing by James Seymour, 1752